PRAISE FOR

"Victor Fuhrman is a very wise
verse. In these pages, you'll discover sonnets of soulmates, odes to daily life, letters to the Divine and gratitude for the gifts of daily life! Victor's words uplift us, even during times of strife. So, when you are ready to celebrate, or in need of a balm for grief, let this book provide clarity, understanding, and relief!"

– Arielle Ford, author of *The Love Thief.*

"When you read Victor Fuhrman's book of poetry, ***Circles and Rings***, you have the pleasure of meeting the hearts and souls of his ancestors. You'll read poems that are jaunty, poems that would make Gilbert & Sullivan chuckle, others that would make a Muppet smile and others that will move your heart or bring a tear to your eye. It's a smorgasbord of poetic delights. Victor's poems are alive with grace, brimming with joy, and topped with love. He will inspire you, move you, tickle you, but never bore you. These are the collected works of a gifted man recounting his life experiences in rhyme and verse seasoned with insight and heart. I highly recommended reading this book and turning down the corners of your favorite poems that you'll want to revisit again and again. ***Circles and Rings*** is a keeper and something special to pass down to the next generation."

– Kac Young, Ph.D., author of 29 books
focused on living your best life.

"I am always amazed at the beautiful yet profoundly meaningful poetry Victor writes. He is even better at reading aloud his clever and transformational poetry. His poems are full of life's teachings, irony, and humor. My favorite poem is "The Power of No," which I now have on my refrigerator door. I could have used this spiritual knowledge years ago and it would have made my life less complicated and more empowering. I am thrilled the world can now experience the soulful words of wisdom and the great wit of my friend, and star brother, Victor Fuhrman."

– Tamara Caulder Richardson, International Evidential and
Psychic Medium known as the Southern Belle Medium®,
Director of The Academy of Divine Wisdom.

"Victor Fuhrman lends his insightful "Voice" in this charming collection of poetic rhythm & rhyme to guide us on life's journey. With humorous anecdotes that recall Dr. Seuss and Shel Silverstein, Fuhrman shares his wholehearted wisdom about the brain inside the heart, healing our inner child, the power of one, and how to "brew" love. He tells us "the magic is in your heart; you just have to make it so." You'll want to keep this book of poems close to your heart."

– Meredith Heller, author of *Writing by Heart* and *Write a Poem, Save Your Life.*

Circles And Rings

5/2/25

Bernie –
MAY we spiral
together for another
interview on your
next book!!

Victor [illegible]

Circles And Rings

A COLLECTION OF POETRY FROM THE SOUL

Victor Fuhrman

Circles and Rings - A Collection of Poetry from the Soul

Publisher: Goddess Communications, LLC
Cover and Interior Design: Qamber Designs and Media

Some of the material in this book was originally presented in Victor Fuhrman's teachings, print articles and social media.

ISBN paperback: 978-1-941630-99-0
ISBN e-book: 978-1-941630-98-3
ISBN audio-book: 978-1-941630-97-6

This book is dedicated to my amazing children, Abby and Alex, and to my beloved wife, partner, muse, and Publishing Goddess, Laurie Sue Brockway, who has blessed my life with her wisdom, presence, and soulmate love!

CONTENTS

ACKNOWLEDGEMENTS

I would like to express my gratitude to all of the teachers that have graced my life and encouraged me to write and share my poetry. I also extend this gratitude to the numerous friends and organizations that have embraced my poetry and shared their feedback as to how it resonated with them on multiple levels, including emotionally and spiritually. Special recognition is offered to The New Seminary and The Interfaith Temple, the organizations that blessed my life in more ways than I can express. For those interested, The New Seminary may be contacted through their website, https://new-seminary.org/, and The Interfaith Temple at https://theinterfaithtemple.org/.

I have come to understand that poetry, and all forms of art, have a genetic component. This was evident by the family of poets, The Fuhrman family, into which I was born. My father, Abe Fuhrman, his brother, my uncle Will, and sisters, my aunts Ada Steinberg and Lillian Laster, were all poets in their own right. They inspired me to express my visions and inspirations in writing. I will be forever grateful for the "gift of rhyme" that I inherited from them, and the understanding that even "silly" and "capricious" words are acceptable in the art of poetry, as long as they come from the heart.

My ultimate acknowledgement goes to my beloved wife, partner, and soulmate, Laurie Sue Brockway. She inspires me in everything I do, and encouraged me as I assembled and published this collection.

INTRODUCTION

As I mentioned in my acknowledgements, my father and his siblings were all poetic if not published poets. I remember family get togethers in the mid to late 1950's when I was six or seven years old, and when the children were asked to leave the room and play, I would sneak back and hide so that I could hear them exchanging jokes and limericks. Of course, limericks were usually vulgar but I loved the rhyming! I would often spend time visiting my aunts and uncles. I remember Aunt Ada playing showtunes on the piano and encouraging me to sing along and even make up alternate rhyming lyrics. Aunt Lillian was a stock broker, and while staying with her during the summer, she took me to the office. I was fascinated by the "stock ticker" and the names of the companies. I started making note of the names and some of the terms used in stock trading in those days, (the early to mid-1960's), and actually composed a blues lyric entitled "The Stock Market Syndrome." I remember one of the lines--"All of my sources have been my remorse's, I'm losing." Later, she composed a tune on her piano and we laughed as I sang my lyrics.

In my early teens, I would receive "downloads" of rhymes and write them into early poetry, including "Injustice" which I discuss in part one, Me and Poe.

My spiritual path reopened in my late thirties with yoga, meditation and retreats, and much of my adult poetry started to flow then. Considering that my "day job" was in welding technology, the spiritual side of life provided a wonderful opportunity to be inspired and share those inspirations as poems.

One of the adult callings on my spiritual journey led me to a wonderful organization, The New Seminary. It was one of the first interfaith seminaries, founded by Rabbi Joseph Gelberman and other interfaith luminaries such as Swami Satchidananda. Many of my spiritual and interfaith poems were engendered by this experience.

The title poem of this book, "Circles and Rings," came to me after the passing of my mother in January of 2020. I officiated her funeral and while doing so began to see a vision of circles and rings and it planted the seeds for this poem.

After her passing, I was going through some of her paperwork and belongings, and I found a series of love poems my father had written for her both before and after they were married. This confirmed what I had thought about the gift of poetry being passed down in our family's genes.

In 2020, I was contacted by The New Seminary and returned to receive my Doctorate in Spiritual Direction. I was also called to join the ministry staff of The Interfaith Temple as Minister of Communications and participated in on-line services until 2022. I contributed both song lyrics and poems to the services as well as occasional sermons and messages.

Again, poetry for me has always been inspired. I see poetry as a form of literary alchemy. I'm grateful for this familial "inheritance," and invite you to join me on this magical journey!

PART ONE
IN THE BEGINNING

EDGAR ALLAN POE

ME AND POE – INJUSTICE

When I was a child in the early 1960's, I was obsessed with the writing of Edgar Allan Poe. I actually thought at one point that I may have been Poe in a previous incarnation! When I was twelve, the following poem came through me after a dream which reinforced the Poe connection.

Injustice (1965)

The blocks were closed around my neck,
The splintered hole burned my neck sore.
The blade would come tumbling to my neck,
And I would see daylight no more.

The King has summoned me to death,
He said that I had been disloyal.
Soon I would swallow my last breath,
To end a life of stress and toil.

And now the black-masked man he comes,
To release the blade of destiny....
T'was not the blade that gave me death,
The crime of injustice gave death to me.

HUMOR

PART TWO
POETIC HUMOR

FAMILY COURTESY

A lesson I learned as a child in the 1950's and shared with my daughter and son in a humorous but practical way!

Family Courtesy (And Manners for Kids of All Ages)

If you open doors and drawers
While coming, going, or doing chores,
Keep this poem to remind you
Kindly shut them all behind you!

If you finish the milk or juice
Then you will have no excuse,
Let them know that they need more
So they can buy it at the store!

When using a towel for bath or shower
Also use your superpower!
Put a fresh one on the rack
So others may dry front and back!

If you use up all the TP
While number two-ing or making pee-pee,
Please replace that precious roll
So other folks may use the bowl!

Courtesy is my advice
If you want folks to think you're nice,
And if you want them to top rank you
Use the magical words, please and thank you!

3

DOCENT LIMERICKS

I love word play and puns, and sometimes have a wicked, if abstract, sense of humor. A few years ago, I started hearing the word docent rather frequently and was intrigued by it. For those not familiar, a docent is someone who volunteers as a guide or instructor at museums and art galleries. Occasionally they receive a stipend, but most of the time do it for the love of the experience. In any event, the word docent became ever present in my "silly word" lexicon and I have crafted three limericks using it. I wanted to write twelve, but you will have to be satisfied with a quarter of a docent. Feel free to groan, and just know this is a form of therapy for me.

A curator whose budget was low
Sought a guide who would handle his show
In the square dance museum
A good guide would free him
And he'd pay 'em with docent dough

A larcenous docent named Ventury
Thought his theft would be less evidentiary
But he was mistaken
And found himself shaken
When charged with the crime of docentury

A wise-ass young tour guide named Dozier
Wanted ladies to lose their composure
He appeared in the buff
But they called his bluff
He was charged with indocent exposure

Thanks for your human docency!

SHOULDA

A while back, someone mentioned something they had not completed and said, "I shoulda." This brought back to memory the old expressions, "shoulda, coulda, woulda." I thought to myself, this would make a great poem! Then I realized the scarcity of words that would rhyme with this. I normally compose at least three stanzas for each poem. For this one, I struggled and used "poetic license" to come up with two. I shoulda....well, not going there!

Shoulda

Sometimes we have regrets for decisions left unmade,
Sometimes we have regrets for debts left unpaid.
Sometimes we choose the wrong horse
out of the remuda, (look it up)
And all of these may lead us to say the shoulda, coulda, woulda.

Don't dwell on things undone, as that time has passed,
Act on the here and now, and your goals will be surpassed.
Be mindful in the present, the teaching of the Buddha,
And you'll never have to chant the shoulda, coulda, woulda.

PART THREE
FOR THE CHILDREN

BRAIN INSIDE THE HEART

A couple of years ago, I read that the heart actually has its own nervous system that some call the "heart brain" or "intrinsic cardiac nervous system". That inspired this reflection.

The Brain Inside the Heart

We all know the brain inside our head,
That's supposed to make us smart.
But very few know or have even read,
About the brain inside our heart.

The brain in the heart is very small,
But is much smarter than the other.
It is the most sensitive brain of all,
When we connect with one another.

The brain in the heart can feel things,
In its own very special way.
It always knows when truth rings,
Or when we have gone astray.

If we learn to listen when it speaks,
We can make our lives the best.
And navigate its valleys and peaks,
With love and joy and zest.

So always listen to your heart,
And everything that it tells you.
You'll know what to do right from the start,
And its wisdom will always bless you.

6

CHILD OF MY SPIRIT

Recognizing that sometimes we harbor a hurt and frightened inner child, this poem came as a form of comfort for me and those who resonate with the message.

Child of My Spirit

Child of my spirit, why do you cry?
My arms will enfold you as you tell me why.
Share all your dreams, your hopes and your fears,
As my love is the tissue to dry all your tears.

Child of my spirit, it's time to heal.
Know that you're loved and that love is real.
Let go of the doubts that you've carried since birth,
And know that you're precious as gold in your worth.

Child of my spirit, it's time to shine.
Open your heart and all will be fine.
Trust that your path is steady and true
And know The Divine will always love you.

PART FOUR
THE GIFT OF ENERGY

IS IT RIGHT FOR YOU?

One of my teachings has been using our subtle senses when presented with decisions. That teaching inspired this poem.

Is It Right For You?

We are presented with so many choices in life,
Some bringing joy, some leading to strife.
To welcome the best, and make others few,
How may you know what is right for you?

The first way is clairvoyance, the special sight,
The ability to see if it's wrong or it's right.
With spiritual eyes, and a vision that's clear,
Seeing the right way from far and from near.

The second is clairaudience, the inner voice,
Using spiritual ears, before making the choice.
And a message that's both insightful and true,
Hearing the answer that's right for you.

The third is clairsentience, the way that it feels,
Energetically knowing what's right and what's real.
True feeling within, and feeling without,
"Clear feeling" will help you erase any doubt.

And along with these "clairs," there are a few more,
We may use them when choosing to open a door.
And trusting these senses, when change is in view,
Gifts for knowing what is best and right for you.

8

MAKE IT SO

I always loved when Sir Patrick Stewart as "Captain Picard" on "Star Trek: The Next Generation" would give commands to the helm by saying, "Make it so!" That phrase inspired this poem.

Make It So

The power is yours, it lies within,
You just must let it go.
And it is so easy to begin,
Simply open and make it so.

Energy guided with intention,
With awareness for you to bestow.
Transcend to the higher dimension,
With desire you make it so.

Learn to trust your inner voice,
It says what you need to know.
You are always free to make the choice,
With freedom you make it so.

The magic key is in your heart,
When it's opened the love will flow.
Know you're worthy right from the start,
With love you make it so!

THE POWER OF ONE

While attending a yoga and meditation retreat with dear friends and teachers, I began visualizing mathematical exponents (powers). I realized that the collective energy of our group, and potentially humanity, would manifest unity, The Power of One. From 1989.

The Power of One

The energy flows from the love of the sun and charges a soul,
The power of one.

That energy shared with a spirit that's new, a heart opens up,
The power of two.

Ebbing and flowing between women and
men, hearts on the wavelength,
The power of ten.

And when all of the millions with compassion
run, the birth of the new mind,
The power of one.

PART FIVE
HEALING POEMS

WHO ARE THE HEALERS?

A friend asked me, "What does it take to be a healer?" That question inspired my response and this poem.

Who Are The Healers?

Those who truly listen and hear…
Those who comfort and dry the tear…

Those who nourish the body and mind…
Those who are always grateful and kind…

Those who are ready to share a smile…
Those who will go that extra mile…

Those who see each other as whole…
Those who see each other as soul…

Who are the healers? We are the healers!

BROKEN

I've been blessed with the gift of being "handy," with mechanical aptitude and the ability to repair just about anything. Thinking about this inspired this poem about fixing that which is "broken" in our lives, not with tools or spare parts, but with reflection, self-compassion, and love.

Broken

From time to time, we all may feel broken,
By challenges, loss, and words unspoken.
And although these things may lead to despair,
With life and faith, there is always repair.

No tools are needed to make this fix,
No parts, nor manuals, or video tricks.
Just the true knowing that things will heal,
With clearest intentions, and energy real.

So when that feeling of "broken" sets in,
Take a slow deep breath and go within.
And visualize the path to heal and to mend,
And know in your heart, you'll be whole again!

12

THE HEALING POWER OF NO

My childhood relationship with my father engendered the sense that if you take care of others, you will be loved. I became a "people pleaser" following this, ultimately resulting in my own health issues being neglected. This led to an awakening in my fifties and the creation of healthy boundaries. I learned that it was okay to say "no" when my energy was being usurped and to only say "yes" when appropriate. That inspired this poem.

The Healing Power of "No"

A time comes for choosing,
Rather than losing
The essence that makes us so.
And in the bestowing,
There's power in knowing
The freedom that comes with "No."

When said with compassion,
Not angry in fashion
And letting the self-love flow.
There's a sense of renewing,
And deep soul imbuing
The awareness that comes with "No."

So with gentle voice,
And the power of choice
And the courage to make it so.
I am still here my friends,
There's no means in this end
Just the healing that comes with "No."

13

THIS SOUL IS NOT FOR SALE

As a healer and coach, I've often shared these spiritual skills pro bono with those in true need. Several years ago, a business friend asked me how I balanced my "day job" in industrial welding with my spiritual work. I responded that the "day-job" paid my salary and the spiritual work paid my Soulary™. At Laurie Sue's urging, I trademarked Soulary™ and my first solo-book after this will be entitled, *Soulary™ : The Compensation of Spirit.*

This Soul Is Not For Sale

I share what I share with open heart,
So that kindness and healing prevail,
For those who say it's not so smart,
This soul is not for sale.

In a world that longs for compassion and love,
Where many are frightened and frail,
What price could there be for comfort thereof?
This soul is not for sale.

"You mean you do what you do, for free?"
Implying my efforts travail,
"Compensation of spirit's my Soulary™,
And this soul is not for sale.

FOR RAVEN KEYES

I had the blessing of meeting Raven Keyes in the summer of 2020. Raven was the founder of Raven Keyes Medical Reiki International, LLC., and the author of *Medical Reiki: A Groundbreaking Approach to Using Energy Medicine for Challenging Treatments.* She worked closely with medical professionals to bring Reiki into hospitals and the operating room. Raven transitioned in May of 2023, and I was inspired to share this poem at her memorial service.

For Raven Keyes

The Raven is said to bridge the worlds of material and spirit,
Our Raven bridged material medicine,
bringing new energy near it.
With her passion she opened the hospital
door, bringing Reiki in,
And the art of Medical Reiki was born, greater healing to begin.

She called to us on the healing path to
embrace her wisdom and ways,
With the compassion and positive energy
that Medical Reiki conveys.
She diligently showed the doctors, how
their patients would heal and thrive,
And that combing the best of both healing
worlds would result in better lives.

Our beautiful Raven has taken flight
and soars free in a higher place,
Welcomed and loved for all she's done
with determination and grace.
We'll never forget her precious gifts and
loving ways from the start,
And as she flies free we will always hold
her golden Keyes in our hearts.

RESURRECTION

This poem was inspired for those going through major life changes to remind them of their worth and that they are loved.

Resurrection

Rebirth is always within our reach,
Not some far off or lofty goal.
Not an illusion or figure of speech,
But a birthright within every soul.

It's not about absolution of sin,
Or seeking far reaching perfection.
It's affirming the wholeness that lies within,
That's the key to our resurrection.

Open your heart to your higher self,
You are loved and it's always been so.
Know you are worthy and love yourself,
You're reborn in the moment you know.

PART SIX
CARING AND COMPASSION

SHARED TEARS

There was a period of time in the early 1990's when several friends lost family members.
This poem came through me then and has resonated many times in the ensuring years. The "green wheel" refers to the heart chakra.

Shared Tears

Welling up from inside as the green wheel spins free,
And the pathway reopens with life energy.
The release of the pain or the joy or the fear,
Or a newly found truth in a miracle year.

As the gates open wide and emotions run free,
And we question the blessing or curse with, "why me?"
The support of two arms makes the burden so light,
A touch, a caress or embrace, so tight.

For the burden is lighter and the truth more profound,
And the joy is much greater when a sharer is found.
And the day is much brighter, and the path quickly clears,
When two become one in the way of shared tears.

I SHARE YOUR PAIN

Inspired by the loss and change during the COVID Pandemic.

I Share Your Pain

For those who've lost jobs and careers
And are striving to maintain,
I share all of your hopes and fears
And yes, I share your pain.

For those whose lives are now on hold
And from gathering must refrain,
I know that life may feel empty and cold
And yes, I share your pain.

For those who've lost their mom or dad
And in grieving now remain,
I share your tears and know how sad
And yes, I share your pain.

For those who see our country shake
And hatred's awful stain,
I know that hearts have come awake
And yes, I share your pain.

For those who pray that this will end
And love will rule again,
I pray with you, my dearest friend
And yes, I share your pain.

THE GIFT OF TRUE LISTENING

Did you ever wish someone would just listen to you, without interruption, when sharing your upset or problems. This poem addresses this very important gift.

The Gift of True Listening

There often are words
That need to be heard
Without cutting in or positioning.
Your heart will be stirred
And compassion conferred
As you offer the gift of true listening.

You'll create sacred space
While bestowing great grace
With love all around you glistening.
It may be any place
Where a soul you embrace
As you offer the gift of true listening.

So, gift someone near you
By saying, "I hear you,"
Lifting them up with your christening.
And one day when you're due
You will be heard too
Receiving the gift of true listening.

SIMPLE GIFTS – THE 3 L'S

Several years ago, I was musing about the greatest gifts we might share with each other rather than the material gifts so often associated with birthdays, anniversaries and holidays. This inspired The Three L's

Simple Gifts – The Three L's

There are three simple gifts we may offer each other,
Priceless when shared with our sisters and brothers.
Gifts from the heart that will serve us all well,
And each of these starts with the twelfth letter, "L."

The first gift is Listening, without opining or word,
Truly listening to and hearing, those who need to be heard.
Compassionate listening to someone that is near you,
And touching their soul by saying, "I hear you."

The second gift is Looking with eyes of compassion,
Truly seeing our oneness, in this human fashion.
Recognizing our unity, in this world that we share,
And using our eyes to show that we care.

The third gift is Loving, the most precious of all,
Opening our hearts and following love's call.
First loving within us, and then loving without,
The finest gift loving, of this there's no doubt.

And these gifts won't be found in market nor store,
Can't be bought for a hundred, a thousand, or more.
They're endowed to us all by the divine up above,
The lesson to listen, to look, and to love.

INDEPENDENCE – INTERDEPENDENCE

This came through me on July 4th several years ago as I sat outside, admiring nature, and recognizing the interdependence of everything.

Independence — Interdependence

There is a song of Nature that she proudly sings,
The "interdependence" of all living things.
From the simplest of life to complex design,
The keys to existence within intertwined.

All beings that breath the oxygen from air,
Exhale carbon dioxide that plant-life will share.
And when plants and trees process the carbon,
They give back the oxygen as part of the bargain.

Our animal companions that we adore,
Four-legged, two-legged, winged, and more.
Depend on us for nourishment and care,
And we are nourished by the love that they share.

And think of the things we two-leggeds do,
We need one another, and this is so true.
With our unique gifts that we share with others,
Sustaining the lives of our sisters and brothers.

So take a few minutes and extend your gratitude,
Appreciate each other, with kind loving attitude.
And as we celebrate this Day of Independence,
Let us not forget our human Interdependence.

BREWING

What kind of "brew" may everyone enjoy, all year round?

Brewing

There's a kind of brew we may all prepare,
Without water, hops or yeast.
It's made with tender loving care,
For all to enjoy and feast.

Suitable for the young and the old,
There is no age limitation.
Brewed for all tastes, sweet to bold,
Touched with imagination.

The recipe for this amazing brew,
One ingredient is all that's needed.
A kettle full of love and a stir or two,
And your brew master's task succeeded.

AWARENESS, KINDNESS, AND GRATITUDE

I've been blessed with opportunities to share what I have learned and experienced with young co-workers and interns that I have trained. This poem was inspired by an actual question one of these interns asked me.

Awareness, Kindness, and Gratitude

A young man asked me, as if to task me
From where I derived my calm attitude.
I smiled so gently and shared contently
"From awareness, kindness and gratitude."

He seemed perplexed and a little bit vexed
And asked if this was just platitude.
I smiled again and told my young friend
"Just awareness, kindness and gratitude."

I extended my hand, to this puzzled young man
Knowing youth often grows through great latitude.
Then he gently smiled and his gaze turned mild
With awareness, kindness and gratitude.

SEEDS OF LOVE

This is a lyric that I wrote for the Interfaith Temple that was set to music and beautifully performed by my dear friend and colleague, Rev. Dr. Samora Smith.

Seeds of Love

We plant seeds to grow trees,
With roots deep in the ground.
We plant seeds to grow blooms,
Their beauty abounds.
We plant seeds to grow grains,
With which we make bread.
We plant seeds to grow fruit,
Our family they're fed.

Chorus
And there are seeds that we plant,
In each other's hearts.
We sow them with songs,
We sow them with arts.
We sow them words,
That come from above.
Our most precious planting,
We sow Seeds of Love.

We plant seeds to build homes,
With comfort and care.
We plant seeds full of hope,
For our children to share.
We plant seeds of renewal,
With kindness in mind.
We plant seeds of compassion,
Great healing to find.

Repeat Chorus

CHILD BECOMES THE PARENT

I wrote and shared this on Mother's Day 2017 for all of us caring for our moms and for those very special moms we care for. Happy Mother's Day to all moms, past, present and future!

When the Child Becomes the Parent

She gave me life and delivered me, into this wondrous world
She took my hand and guided me, as the mysteries unfurled.
She taught me to be loving, and all the time she smiled
Now the child becomes the parent and the parent, the child.

She encouraged me to study, and learn all that I could
She taught me to be confident, while doing what was good.
She urged me to have faith, when life's challenges beguiled
Now the child becomes the parent and the parent, the child.

She taught me to be compassionate, a most important teaching
She taught me loving kindness, her gift was future reaching.
As now she needs these back from me, as lost memories are filed
For the child has become the parent and the parent, the child.

9-11

Laurie Sue and I served as chaplains for the Red Cross in the aftermath of 9-11. It was a time of unity and caring. In the ensuing years, much of this has sadly been forgotten. It is my prayer that we remember. (From 2021)

9-11

Sometimes it takes a tragedy, to remind us of our unity,
It brings out what is best in every person and community.
We all embrace each other, as one great extended family,
With compassion and support and embracing inclusivity.

One such event united us, just twenty years ago,
When unthinkable inhumanity, dealt a deadly blow.
In the aftermath we bonded, and emerged with great resolve,
And for a brief and shining moment, our nation did evolve.

And we grieved the loss together, honoring our dead,
Exalting brave responders, who sacrificed in our stead.
And lauding those who answered the call, our enemy to find,
A truly united nation, one America, one mind.

And politics were put aside, for the benefit of us all,
Our leaders were working together, responding to our call.
They might not have always all agreed, but did their very best,
To serve those who elected them, at a time of fear and test.

And twenty years have come and gone, and unity diminished,
Dissention, division, and argument,
with compromising finished.
The common good, a thing of the past, while angry voices shout,
A people forsaken by those they trust, left with fear and doubt.

The greatest tragedy manifests, when people forget their past,
Forget the meaning of fellowship and how to make it last.
May we come together once again,
united as sisters and brothers,
May we remember that shining moment,
and care for one another.

UBUNTU – I AM BECAUSE WE ARE

In preparing a sermon on unity for The Interfaith Temple, I came across the word "Ubuntu" that inspired this poem.

Ubuntu — I Am Because We Are

In many nations of Africa, there is a special word,
Across dialogues and languages, it's meaning may be heard.
Embracing all of humanity, in places near and far,
The message woven within this word, "I am because we are."

For Bantu Zulu people, the famous word, "Ubuntu",
In Kenya's many tongues, "Utu", "Munto" and "Umundu."
In Malawi and Zambia, the people say "Umunthu,"
In Angola and the Congo, expressed there as "Gimunto."

The philosophy these people share is one of great community,
A universal bond of sharing, connecting all humanity.
Where villages will welcome you as part of greater family,
And their children are embraced by all, as their responsibility.

Ubuntu is a way of life, to which all should aspire,
A unity of humanity, fueled by compassion's fire.
With a spirit of loving kindness, the world we may imbue,
With the wisdom that Ubuntu and Unity, both begin with you!

ONE SIMPLE RULE

In my interfaith studies, I discovered that there is an iteration of "The Golden Rule" in virtually every faith. This poem expresses my hope that we all recognize each other as sisters and brothers and follow this one simple rule.

One Simple Rule

One simple rule, in every faith, may easily be found,
In every language, everywhere, with wisdom so profound.
Understanding, that at our core, we are all the same,
We simply need, to join our voices, the rule we shall proclaim.

You are my neighbor, and my friend, in you I also see me,
I will embrace you, my sister and brother, as my true family.
And treat you with loving kindness, as I would receive from you,
And honor our humanity, our oneness I know is true.

And so this rule we live by, has a very special name,
So simple, yet so precious, a bright eternal flame.
As we do unto each other, with compassion and great love,
This simple rule is golden, endowed by the divine above.

PART SEVEN

NATURE POEMS

OLIVER THE SQUIRREL

A frequent visitor inspired this squirrel tail!

Oliver the Squirrel

A squirrel lives in our mulberry tree,
He visits us every day.
When he stands by our door we're filled with glee,
And there's something he seems to say!

He loves when we give him snacks and treats,
Especially filberts and figs.
He always takes two and then he retreats,
Comes back and dances a jig!

And then he does something really smart,
He raises his front paws and begs.
The look in his eyes just opens your heart,
As he stands waiting on his hind legs!

He reminds us of young Oliver Twist,
As he patiently waits with ease.
And he seems to ask with bent paws and wrists,
"Sir, may I have some more, please?"

MOLLY THE SPIDER

This chance encounter actually took place outside of our home. Although shared humorously, I had a true connection with this beautiful little arachnid.

Miss Molly The Spider

Next to our house there's a green fence,
And a pathway that runs there beside her.
It was there on that fence, with a little suspense,
That I first met Miss Molly, The Spider.

She weaved her first web from the fence to the door,
Not knowing that we have to pass there.
And I almost tripped and fell to the floor
Avoiding a wrecked-web disaster!

So me and Miss Molly, to avoid one more folly,
Had an eight eye to two eye mind meeting.
With arachnid compassion, in a fashion so crawly,
We shared mental pictures, quite fleeting.

Without word or sound, the result so profound,
As we both agreed to abide there.
Her webs to one side, and the door out of bounds,
I made peace with Miss Molly, The Spider!

LESSON OF THE AZALEAS

Witnessing the return of the gorgeous annual Azaleas in our small front garden inspired this poem and served to help me during a time of grief.

Lesson of the Azaleas

They return each spring, in their full glory,
Without our hand in tending.
Leave in three weeks, a very short story,
But no sadness in this ending.

For they grace us with signs, of summer's return,
Lifting our spirits with cheer.
And we know they'll be back, and blossom again,
One full turn of the wheel of the year.

And the lesson they share, with beauty and grace,
Transition is just nature's way.
A reminder we all will return to this place,
And blossom on some shining day!

PART EIGHT
INTERFAITH POEMS

SACRED DANCE

This is another poem that I composed to share at the Interfaith Temple. I recognized sacred dance as universal in so many religions and cultures as a way of expressing faith in the Divine.

Sacred Dance

It started with raising our hands to the sky,
Or kneeling and touching the ground.
Receiving the blessings from spirit on high,
Or praying with insight profound.

Some worshiped the sun in their sacred dance,
Waving their arms to-and-fro.
And at night with great fires, sure to entrance,
Circling flames and the embers that glow.

Temple dancers undulated and swayed,
Seeking Greco-Roman deities' favor.
While harps and lyres and flutes were played,
Both divine and the humans to savor.

In India, sacred dances were found,
In the great Sanskrit text, Natyashastra.
Delicate movements and mudras abound,
Epic stories performed from the Sastras.

Tribal dancers honor Mother Earth,
Giving thanks for all animals and crops.
True recognition of all nature's worth,
Rhythmic gratitude that never stops.

And today we dance as a form of prayer,
Giving thanks for our lives and our souls.
With love and grace, awareness, and care,
The Glory of the Divine it extolls.

HERE I AM AND I AM READY

While attending The New Seminary (Interfaith) in the mid 1990's, the founder, Rabbi Joseph Gelberman, shared the Hebrew word "Hineni." He taught that the literal translation was "Here I Am" but that spiritually it also meant, "I am ready." That teaching resonated with me and inspired this poem.

Hineni — Hear I Am and I Am Ready

An ancient calling, from The Divine
From desert sands to holy shrine
Answered clear, answered steady
"Here I Am, and I Am Ready."

Called to Abraham, a test of devotion
Called to Moses, set freedom in motion
Called to Isaiah, "Who can I send?"
Calls to us all, our world to mend.

I heard the call, to serve and heal
To do what's right, to do what's real
With full presence, and spirit steady
Here I Am, and I Am Ready.

THE MESSENGERS

Inspired by Interfaith study and learning.

The Messengers

Delivering words from The Divine,
Reassuring the faithful all will be fine.
Found in so many faiths and beliefs,
Blessed assurance to bring them relief.

From Abraham to Moses, Isaiah to Daniel,
"God is with us" the word is Emmanuel.
The birth of a deliverer as it was foretold,
With tidings of comfort and saving of souls.

And Miriam, Deborah, Mary and Joan,
Women of courage, their wisdom was shown.
In word and in deed, great messengers all,
Ready to answer the Divine's holy call.

And later in lineage, another one came,
The "Seal of the Prophets," Muhammad his name.
Received from Jibril, the way of Islam,
And brought to the Muslims, the Holy Quran.

The Seventh Avatar of Vishnu, Lord Rama his name,
The forces of darkness, his dharma to tame.
His great story of victory, defeating Ravana,
Cherished by Hindus, the great "Ramayana."

In Patna Sahib from lineage Sikh, was born Gobinda Rai,
The final Sikh Guru in human form, would lift his people high.
As Gobind Singh he delivered the word,
Sikhs follow to this very day,
And established the creed of Singh Khalsa,
"The Lions" of faith in their way.

A Persian preacher, known as the Báb,
saw a new prophet emerging,
Bahá'u'lláh heard the call and followed Divine spirit's urging.
Despite persecution, exile and detention,
his words of unity thrived,
And they birthed a faith of inclusion
and love, known as the Bahá'í.

And messengers come to guide us each
day, if we but choose to hear,
In the form of friends or spirit guides, or angels soft and clear.
Or the inner voice of our higher selves,
with guidance from above,
With words of comfort and sound
advice, always shared with love.

A POEM OF PASSOVER

Shared with the Interfaith Temple, Passover 2021.

A Poem of Passover

A child drawn from the water,
A divine plan to unfold.
Raised by Pharoah's daughter,
A prophecy foretold.

A people held in bondage,
Moses' heart could not abide.
From angered Pharoah's sondage,
He had to flee and hide.

Midian offered respite,
And a chance for a new life.
But the Hebrew's lot was desperate,
Filled with suffering and strife.

Knowing his work must be resumed,
The Lord's Glory to Moses did show.
From a burning bush, not consumed,
Tell Pharoah, "Let my people go."

He delivered God's message to Pharoah,
With miracles, wonders, and signs.
The Egyptian King's view was so narrow,
He paid God's commandment no mind.

So, The Lord answered Pharoah's scorn,
With ten mighty and terrible scourges.
And with the death of the first born,
Pharoah's people sang mournful dirges.

He told Moses to take his flock,
And depart old Egypt's land.
They gathered their goods and stock,
And prepared for the desert sand.

Moses told them to be prompt and wise,
That there was no time to waste.
Not even time to let bread rise,
So, they left with the bread of haste.

They began their journey to freedom,
With a sense of deliverance and hope.
And their faith in Moses to lead them,
With each challenge the strength to cope.

But Pharoah's anger grew stronger,
Sending armies to punish and kill.
The Lord would abide him no longer,
His fury to break Pharoah's will.

The Red Sea, the final border,
To leave old Egypt's land.
The Lord gave Moses the order,
To raise his staff in his hand.

The might of The Lord was glorious,
And opened a path cross the sea.
The Hebrews crossed quickly, victorious,
Delivered and finally free.

The Pharoah's army pursued them,
But the Lord let the waters subside.
The crashing waves consumed them,
The great phalanx perished and died.

And the Hebrews praised God and his Glory,
Were grateful for being set free.
And Moses would share their great story,
Passed down through all history.

Years of wandering cleansed them to be so,
With the Commandments of God well in hand.
Moses bid them farewell at Mount Nebo,
And they entered their promised land.

BRICK BY BRICK

This is dedicated to the New Temple, for all peoples, to find love and peace together.

Brick By Brick

Ancient builders sought a new way,
More than nine millennia passed.
They added chopped straw, and sand to clay,
Sun baked them, to make them last.

And when they were dry, strong, and hard,
Joined and aligned with a stick.
Many levels and rows, yard after yard,
They assembled them, brick by brick.

From modest abodes to towering shrines,
They erected them higher and higher.
And when they were called by the Divine,
Great temples designed and inspired.

But even great temples will only stand,
With respect from fellow humanity.
And when soldiers storm, with batters in hand,
Bricks fall in torrential calamity.

And showing great faith, they built once again,
Even greater in stature and splendor.
But as prophesied, their work was in vain,
As the empire's verdict was rendered.

The great prophecy says it will rise again,
When God's people return to their home.
Can this be true, in a world filled with pain,
With so many bereft and alone?

May the builder that dwells in each of our souls,
Embody the spirit of hope.
May we join in this building with our common goals,
That New Shining Temple, our scope.

May The New Temple stand the great test of time,
The architect inside our hearts,
And may we all share in the spirit sublime,
Building with love from the start.

36

REVELATION SONG

Revelation Song

You shared your words,
With prophets of old.
Their hearts were stirred,
The future foretold.

But I need your sign,
As something to feel.
In my heart and my mind,
What will you reveal?

Chorus

You've shown me,
That you're always there.
My faith is the key,
You answer my prayer.
And when I need strength,
You shine your light.
To show me the way,
And make my path bright.

I see your hand,
In all that is good.
In sky and on land,
In ocean and wood.

Your message is clear,
Revealed from the start.
I've nothing to fear,
With you in my heart.

Repeat Chorus

QUAN YIN

One of the lovely chants shared during they yoga classes I began attending in the 1980's was "Om Mani Padme Hum." This translates as "Hail the Jewel in the Lotus" and refers to the Bodhisattva, Quan Yin. Bodhisattva's have earned Nirvana (paradise) but remain within our realm to help us reach enlightenment and freedom. My wife, Laurie Sue Brockway, is an expert on the feminine divine and we have several statues of Quan Yin in our home. This poem was inspired by those statues and the message of The Bodhisattva.

Quan Yin

She completed all of her karma,
Nirvana to be her new home.
So compassionate was her dharma,
That she vowed not to leave us alone.

She saw human kind as her charges,
Stayed to free all from suffering and fear.
The promise of Quan Yin enlarges,
To love all and dry every tear.

The great chant will make us take notice,
Her compassion and love in full bloom.
"Hail the Jewel in the Lotus,"
"Om Mani Padme Hum."

IT'S ALL ABOUT THE LIGHT

This poem was inspired by my time at the New Synagogue, part of the New Seminary, and first shared there at a service in December 2011. It expresses an interfaith approach to "The Season of Light."

It's All About the Light

From ancient times, this holy month,
observed and long remembered
Kislev and Dongzhi on lunar paths, and
the Roman Sun's December.
The golden threads of the holy days form a tapestry so bright....
And the eternal message woven therein,
"It's All About the Light!"

Those who followed nature's path and worshiped sky and earth,
Burned altar candles and chanted prayers
awaiting the Sun's rebirth.
The fires of Yule danced against the sky,
shielding them from the night,
And they exclaimed as Sol returned to the
sky, "It's All About the Light."

Antiochus, the Seleucid king, defiled the temple and altar,
The Maccabees, with "hammers" in hand,
pushed back and did not falter.

The Menorah oil, a mere one day's supply,
burned eight holy nights,
The grateful Jews proclaimed with joy,
"It's All About the Light."

On the 8th day of Dongzhi, Gautama sat under the Pipal tree
He awakened and saw the Middle Path as the end of all misery.
He understood non-attachment as a cure for the human plight
When asked how, he said, "I am awake"
and "It's All About the Light."

A male child born to a virgin, the promise the prophets foretold,
"And he shall be as God with us" and savior of lost souls.
A shepherd to a thirsty flock that he kept within his sight
"Peace on Earth and Goodwill Toward
Men", "It's All About the Light."

Love

PART NINE
LOVE POEMS

I LOVED YOU, I LOST YOU, I'LL FIND YOU AGAIN

This is the first of my soulmate writings, inspired by my beloved wife, Laurie Sue.

I Loved You, I Lost You, I'll Find You Again

It all started back when time began,
I loved you, I lost you, and I'll find you again.
Life after lifetime, somewhere and when,
I loved you, I lost you, and I'll find you again…

Captured your beauty with paper and pen,
I loved you, I lost you, and I'll find you again.
Eyes like the deep woods, song like the wren,
I loved you, I lost you, and I'll find you again…

A heart beats behind me, I turn 'round and then,
I loved you, I lost you, and I'll find you again.
Your sweet face is smiling, like when it began,
I loved you, I lost you, and I've found you again!

SOULMATE SONG

This was a lyric that came through me when thinking about soul mate relationships and how they evolve.

Soul Mate Song

Lift your hand up, reach it out before you
There's someone who adores you, right before your eyes.
Lift your hand up; join your hand with my hand,
That's the way it was planned, vision of the wise.

Lift your feet up, walk along a new path
Find your soul's own true path, it's not very far.
Lift your feet up, you and I will meet up,
On some celestial street up, near our shining star.

We have yearned to find each other
In each new soul we'd discover,
But that "I'm home" feeling'd quickly fade
I've dreamed of the day I'd find you,
Open my heart to remind you,
Of the pledge we made in heaven
On that special day.

Lift your hand up, reach it out before you
There's someone who adores you, right before your eyes.
Lift your hand up; join your hand with my hand,
That's the way it was planned, vision of the wise.

Lift your heart up, love has finally found you
It's been all around you, as you now can see.
Lift your heart up; join your heart with my heart,
Let us make a new start, soaring, joyous, free!

MY BELOVED

The first iteration of this poem came through when Laurie Sue turned sixty. As the years ensued, I added her future amazing accomplishments! This is the latest version.

My Beloved

My beloved turns sixty-seven today,
And she is sexy in every way!
From her stellar achievements that continue to grow,
And her quiet devotions that very few know.

She's an author, editor, and publishing star
Whose books have touched hearts, near and far.
From sexy to practical, wise and sage,
Her readers are enchanted by every page.

A master reporter who gets all the facts,
With devotion to truth, ethics and tact.
Her articles and features, insightful and fun,
Broach every subject under the sun.

To the couples she marries of every ilk,
With wisdom, and humor, and words spun like silk.
She weaves faiths and cultures and traditions with ease,
With interfaith skills, all peoples to please.

A Master of History, Public and Such
Who shares written and oral with sensitive touch.
Devoted to sharing the Feminine Divine,
Empowering women to step forward and shine.

A devoted mother, sister and wife,
She works tirelessly to ensure a good life.
She gives so much, often without rest,
So the ones that she loves will receive her best.

From her smile that beguiles and first took my heart,
To the twinkle in her eyes when she's sassy and smart.
From her sensuous sensibilities, so hard to miss,
And her passionate embrace and all-telling kiss.

My beloved turns sixty-seven today,
And she is sexy in every way!

PART TEN
MATURITY

ODE TO A HANDFUL OF NUTS

I had weight reduction surgery in the early 2010's and one of the things that my doctor recommended when I felt hungry was a handful of nuts. It worked!

Ode to a Handful of Nuts

When you watch your girly figure or your very manly vigor,
There can be no ifs, ands or buts.
For the snack that you should favor and
the flavor you should savor,
Should be a healthy little handful of nuts.

Nuts are very handy and so much better than candy,
Filled with good protein and fiber.
A few grams of healthy fat, if you can just imagine that
So even your physician would prescriber. (Poetic License Taken)

So when your stomach tells you, and appetite compels you,
To enjoy a light and healthy repast.
Remember nuts are crunchy, and satisfy your munchies,
And won't add any inches to your ... bottom.
(Poetic License and Cleanliness Taken!)

ODE TO A HARDWOOD FLOOR

We have beautiful, old hardwood floors in our home. The floors in my office are rather worn and I occasionally receive the gift of a splinter as I walk barefoot. That inspired this free verse poem.

Ode to a Hardwood Floor

Born in a forest, you grew to be tall, proud, and free.
Season after season, weathering but not yielding.

Until you were worth more dead than alive
To the men with axes and saws who caused
you to fall into the emerald bed.
With saw and plane, router, and sander
The mill men formed you into their ideal
Rectangular, beveled, joined, precise.
Yet you retained your soul in the knots
and grain they could not erase.
And season after season, weathering but not yielding.

The carpenters measured and cut you and then
mercilessly drove nails through you,
Making you conform to the boundaries of
what pleased their human eyes.
And the finishers came and shaved you
with aluminum and silicon grit.

And in their guilt, soothed your raw flesh with
unguents of mineral spirits and color.
And sometimes you were naked and
sometimes you were clothed,
With weaves of cotton, wool or synthetic skins
And season after season, weathering but not yielding.

You bore the burden of feet and hands and paws,
Of your cousins who became furnishings.
Bore silent witness as you were showered with tears and blood,
The essences of love and our bodily shedding.
And people lived and died, wars were waged and waged again.
The world around you constantly changed,
And season after season, weathering but not yielding.

And now, old friend, we both show signs
of weathering and yielding.
My hair is thinning and brown and silver
while you once again are bare.
The nails that once held you down are snagging at your surface,
As my nails slowly brittle and break
You squeak and flex under my feet and
my knees join your harmony.
Every so often I get a splinter from you just
as I sometimes splinter those I love,
Not deliberately or with mean spirit, just the
result of our growing old and frayed.

And once again you catch my tears as
I mourn the loss of beloveds.
I am grateful to you for sharing my burdens
and silently listening to my pain.
I still see your soul in the knots and grains
that even time cannot erase from you,
And I know that one day, as brothers, we will
both return to the soil that gave us life.

MY MIDDLE NAME

After recently interviewing several wonderful guests for my podcasts, I noticed that many, if not all, had middle names, either expressed as an initial or spelled out. I started reflecting on the fact that I was not given a middle name, not out of a sense of lack, but just wondering what it would be if I had one. Of course, when my wonderment kicks in, a poem is usually not far behind.

My Middle Name

When I was born I was given a name,
Victor, after mom's dad, and the Fuhrman surname.
But there was also something of a riddle,
Between Victor and Fuhrman, 'twas naught in the middle!

Not faulting my parents for leaving this blank,
Nor judging my status for lack of this rank.
But a middle name adds distinction and flair,
And rolls of the tongue as it vibrates the air.

I noticed in marketing a very cute trick,
To make products and services memories stick.
In order for consumers to remember their fame,
They'd say, "Quality" is our middle name."

So what would my middle name be,
To identify something unique about me?
And then I arrived at the obvious choice,
My middle name is simply, "The Voice."

OLD ANCHOR

Several years ago, Laurie Sue officiated a wedding in Baltimore Harbor. While walking the dock, I passed an old ship's anchor that inspired this poem.

Old Anchor

An old anchor rests on a peaceful bay dock,
Sixty years he has been aweigh.
His iron is rusted from crown to his stock,
As he dreams of his shining day.
When his metal was young and his arms were strong,
And his flukes and palms were grand.
He steadied his ship and her souls the day long,
As she docked in many a land.
He knew many a rode and by cathead was stowed,
As his ship traversed ocean and sea.
And when mighty gales blowed, he held tight to his load,
Making sure she would never break free.
But with journeys and age and the turn of the page,
Every story must come to an end.
And this anchor, though sage, earned his pensioner's wage,
And now dreams on this dock, my friend.

PART ELEVEN
SPIRITUAL POEMS

46

SACRED TO ME

A friend inquired about my interfaith path and asked what I considered sacred. This is how I answered.

Sacred to Me

The warmth of the sun upon the face,
A gentle hug or compassionate embrace.
Someone to listen when we need to be heard,
Someone to share their wisdom and word.

The vows of a couple as husband and wife,
The cry of a newborn as it begins life.
The comfort of family as we draw our last breath,
The promise of rebirth vanquishing death.

The glory of nature, earth, sea, and sky,
The beauty of birds as they soar by.
Glorious flowers, green plants, and great trees,
The industrious work of insects and bees.

In each of these things, we see the divine,
The work of creation, all things to align.
Each one a miracle for all eyes to see,
Each one is precious and sacred to me.

47

ASCENSION SONG

Another lyric I composed during my time with The Interfaith Temple. The music was written and vocalized by my dear friend and colleague, Rev. Dr. Samora Smith.

Ascension Song

When we raise our vibration,
The change begins to flow.
It transcends imagination,
As all the feelings grow.

We hear angelic choirs,
As we begin to rise.
We see heavenly spires,
And blue majestic skies.

Chorus
It's the greatest connection,
To love's highest dimension.
It's our soul's true perfection,
That brings about ascension.

When we recognize divinity,
In each and everyone.
Our love reaches infinity,
And our journey has begun.

In the truth of our unity,
We all will start to fly.
A love filled community,
Headed for the sky!

Repeat Chorus

CIRCLES AND RINGS

When my mother passed in January of 2020, I started seeing visions of circles and rings. This poem came through me with an understanding of what I was experiencing and a message that lifted me in my grief.

Circles and Rings

The path of great beauty in so many things,
From atoms to galaxies; circles and rings.
Natural wisdom that dwells there within,
From naught to three-sixty, that magical spin.

We circle each other in gravity's dance,
As Gaia circles Sol; the solar romance.
As Luna circles us in life giving motion,
Drawing the tides, and inner emotion.

And the age of the oak is found in its rings,
As in woman and man, and all living things.
And when the rings stop and life comes to an end,
We'll all circle back, and dance once again.

New Year's Resolutions...

1.
2.
3.

PART TWELVE

TURN OF THE YEAR

49

RESOLUTION REVOLUTION

New Year's Day marks the time that many make resolutions for the coming year. With all of the divisiveness we are experiencing, I sensed it was time for a resolution revolution.

Resolution Revolution

Our resolution revolution,
A path to greater life solutions.
A way to change and find the way,
To make the most of every day.

Resolve to release what does not serve,
Evolve to embrace all we deserve.
Remembering the lessons of posterity,
Recognizing our inner and outer prosperity.

The future is ours to build and share,
With our sisters and brothers everywhere.
Loving ourselves and loving each other,
Loving this Earth, Gaia, our mother.

Revolution because we cannot wait,
Resolved, that fear we must abate.
That trusting, as one, we have the power,
To embody humanity's finest hour.

TURN OF THE YEAR – 2024 AND FOREVER

This poem came through me just before New Year's Day 2024 and reflects my thoughts on the passage of time.

Turn of the Year — 2024 and Forever

Solar and Lunar, counting the days,
Polar, equator, and so many ways.
Some are 360, most 365,
Measuring seasons, the days of our lives.

Some months are warm, others are cold,
Months go too swiftly for those who are old.
Winter to spring, summer to fall,
Childhood, adulthood, seniority's call.

So as old year transitions and new year is born,
We awaken on day one, at first light of dawn.
And resume the great count, turn the new page,
Watch days and months fly, as ever we age.

If we could but stop time, make it relent,
Diminish the worries and energy spent.
And be in the present, through all the years,
Living for now and vanquishing fears....

May your New Year be Joyous, Healthful, and Sweet,
May your path be so gentle, and comfort replete.
May your soul's highest purpose, be in your view,
Dear Friends, my wish, Happy New Year to You....

CLOSING THOUGHTS

Thank you for sharing this poetic journey with me. It is my hope that you found within it something that made you smile (and even laugh), inspired you, warmed your heart, and gave you a sense of soul to soul connection. While sharing these inspired words with different audiences, I've received feedback that many could actually visualize the messages. Some told me that my words were healing and others that they gave them hope. Whatever you took from these pages, I am grateful for your time and interest. Perhaps we will meet again. Thank you, and bless you on your journey.

PHOTO CREDITS

Rings image
Bohdan Populov / Shutterstock.com

Introduction
lhfgraphics / Depositphotos.com

Part One: In The Beginning - Me and Poe – Injustice
Time Trip / Alamy Stock Photo

Part Two: Poetic Humor
dizanna / Depositphotos.com

Part Three: For The Children
Rawpixel / Depositphotos.com

Part Four: The Gift of Energy
rolffimages / Depositphotos.com

Part Five: Healing Poems
healing63 / Depositphotos.com

Part Six: Caring and Compassion
ridofranz / Depositphotos.com

Part Seven: Nature Poems
Azalea taken by the author

Part Eight: Interfaith Poems
crystaleyemedia / Depositphotos.com

Part Nine: Love Poems
andrew.puhach.photo / Depositphotos.com

Part Ten: Maturity
andykazie / Depositphotos.com

Part Eleven: Spiritual Poems
ermess / Depositphotos.com

Part Twelve: Turn of the Year
Wavebreakmedia / Depositphotos.com

ABOUT THE AUTHOR

Reverend Doctor Victor Fuhrman, D.Scd, is a healer, spiritual counselor, and author, whose deep and rich voice inspired the handle, Victor the Voice. With his soulful sound, he helps people heal. He also does this through energy work and ceremony, and is the host and producer of Destination Unlimited, Wednesdays at 8PM EDT and Vox Novus, Thursdays at 8PM EDT, on OmTimes Radio, as well as a contributing editor for OmTimes Magazine. He graduated from and was ordained through the New Seminary in 1997, and received his doctorate from the seminary in 2020. He also served as Minister of Communications for The Interfaith Temple. Reverend Doctor Victor has been marrying couples in love–and counseling people challenged by love, loss, and grief for more than 24 years.

Victor is creator of EnerVision, a curriculum designed to teach psychic self-empowerment and healing with the emphasis on these things being very natural, rather than supernatural. In support of the work of healers across the country, he's been called upon to testify and share his expertise before the White House

Commission on Complementary and Alternative Medicine. He played an important role in helping his spiritual community find healing, spiritual security and feel peaceful in the new world of post 9-11 life in New York City. During that time, he offered meditation groups and spiritual survival counseling and he helped with disaster relief work as a volunteer chaplain for the Red Cross, serving families and rescue workers affected by the World Trade Center attacks.

A former armed forces broadcast journalist, he is a storyteller by nature, and an inspiring public speaker. He brings unconditional love, compassion, and a great sense of humor to his ministry. In addition to his spiritual work and service, he served as Vice President of Sales and Marketing for leading welding and industrial supply distributors in New York, his "day job" for more than 44 years.

He is married to Rev. Laurie Sue Brockway, also a graduate of the New Seminary, and they reside in New York.

PET PRAYERS & BLESSINGS

At least 65% of all American homes include pets, and many owners have begun to recognize the divine nature of all "creatures great and small." This unique collection of blessings specifically addresses the spiritual needs of those modern-day pet owners . Besides offering original prayers and adaptations of classics, it explains how to lead rituals and celebrations, and provides advice on involving pets in spiritual events, including those conducted by the clergy.

Although the work honors many faiths, it is non-denominational and non-religious, and encompasses elements from many cultures and traditions. There are healing prayers for ailing animals, ceremonies for special occasions (such as the arrival of a new pet), and blessings for a long and happy life with your animal companion.

GODDESS COMMUNICATIONS, LLC
NEW YORK CITY

Made in the USA
Middletown, DE
26 April 2025